learn to draw
ANCIENT TIMES

Learn to draw 18 ancient characters and past civilizations

Illustrated by Bob Berry • Written by Sandy Phan

Associate Publisher: Rebecca J. Razo
Art Director: Shelley Baugh
Project Manager: Stephanie Meissner
Senior Editor: Amanda Weston
Production Artists: Debbie Aiken, Amanda Tannen
Production Manager: Nicole Szawlowski
Production Coordinator: Lawrence Marquez
Production Assistant: Janessa Osle

Illustrated by Bob Berry
Written by Sandy Phan

www.walterfoster.com
Walter Foster Publishing, Inc.
3 Wrigley, Suite A
Irvine, CA 92618

1 3 5 7 9 10 8 6 4 2

TABLE OF CONTENTS

GETTING STARTED

When you look closely at the drawings in this book, you'll notice that they're made up of basic shapes, such as circles, ovals, and triangles. To draw the projects in this book, just start with simple shapes as you see here. It's easy and fun!

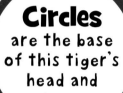
Circles are the base of this tiger's head and legs.

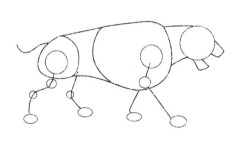 

Rectangles are good for drawing a structure's base.

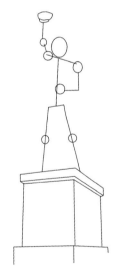 

Triangles are perfect for drawing pyramids.

TOOLS AND MATERIALS

Before you begin, gather some drawing tools, such as paper, a regular pencil, an eraser, and a pencil sharpener. For color, you can use markers, colored pencils, paint, crayons, or even colored chalk.

drawing pencil and paper

eraser

sharpener

colored pencils

felt-tip markers

paintbrush and paints

CAVEMAN

Early human beings lived during the Ice Age.
They slept in caves and hunted with throwing spears.

FUN FACT

Some early humans made art! They painted handprints, symbols, and animals on cave walls using many natural tools. Minerals made different colors, and shells held the paint. They even had assistants to help them mix paints and hold up torches so they could see!

MAMMOTH

Mammoths lived during the Ice Age. They had long tusks and trunks. Woolly mammoths had thick fur to keep them warm.

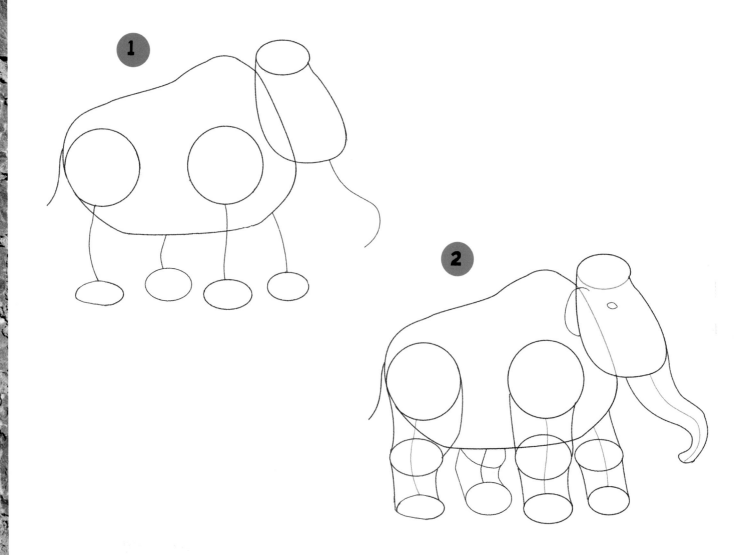

FUN FACT

The word "mammoth" means "huge." Mammoths are related to today's elephants and stood about 10 feet tall at their shoulders. The last mammoths became extinct, or died off, thousands of years ago. We know about them from their bones and cave paintings.

SABER-TOOTHED TIGER

Saber-toothed tigers were named for their teeth that were like sabers: long, curved swords. These prehistoric cats had a deadly bite!

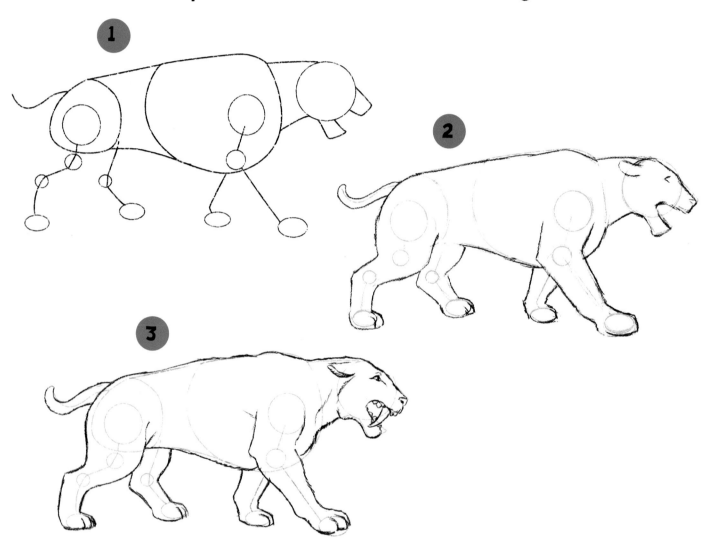

FUN FACT

Saber-toothed tiger and mammoth fossils, or bones, have been found in the La Brea Tar Pits in Los Angeles, California. These Ice Age animals became stuck in the sticky tar and died. The tar kept their bones whole, and scientists study the bones to learn about these extinct animals.

GREAT PYRAMID

The Great Pyramid is the largest of the three Pyramids of Giza in Egypt. Each of its four sides is a triangle.

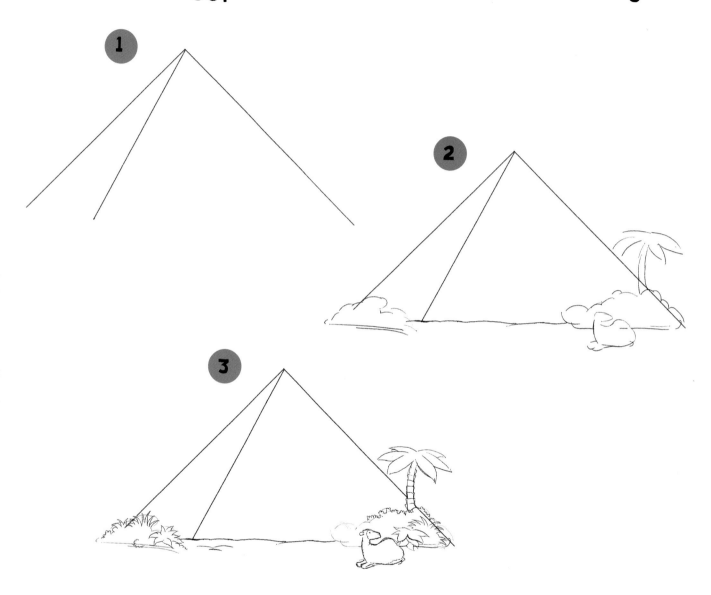

FUN FACT

Pyramids held the bodies of Egyptian kings after they died. The Great Pyramid was built with more than 2 million stone blocks. Each block weighed between 2.5 and 15 tons! It stands at an impressive 451 feet tall.

SPHINX OF GIZA

The sphinx is a mythical creature with a human head and a lion's body. The Sphinx of Giza is a huge statue in Egypt.

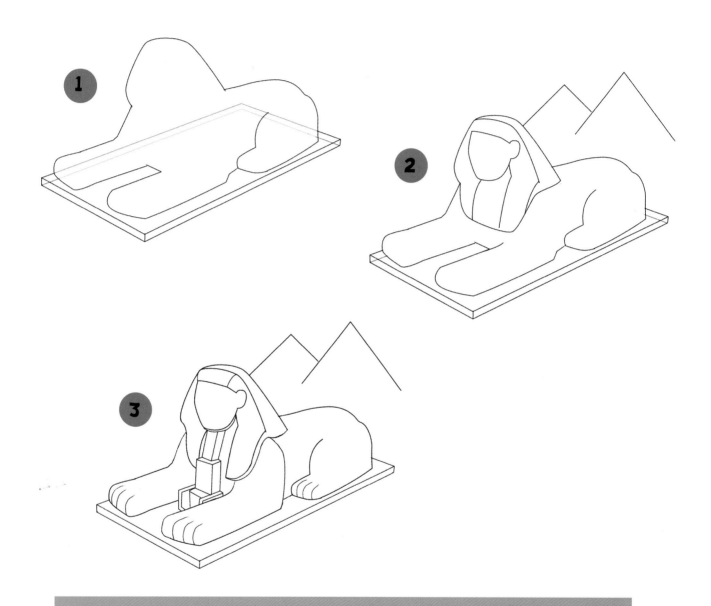

FUN FACT

The Sphinx of Giza was built with the face of King Khafre around 2,500 B.C. Over time, sand buried most of its body. According to legend, prince Thutmose took a nap in the shade of the Sphinx. The Sphinx told him in a dream that he would become king if he unburied it. Thutmose agreed and later ruled Egypt.

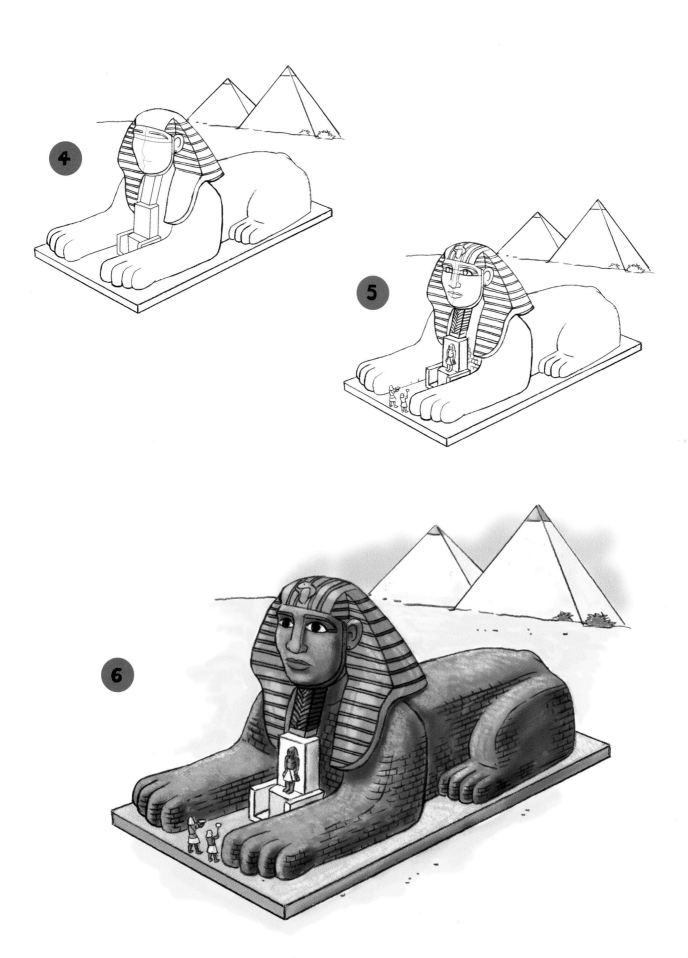

MUMMY

A mummy is a body that is preserved, or kept whole, after death. Making mummies was an acceptable practice in ancient Egypt.

1

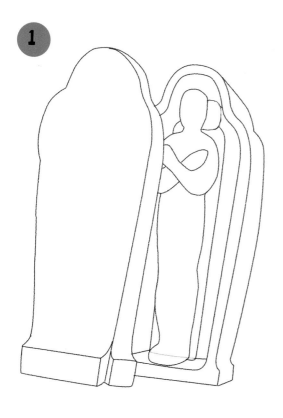

2

DRAWING TIP

Use your crayons, colored pencils, or markers to make your own cool design on the mummy tomb!

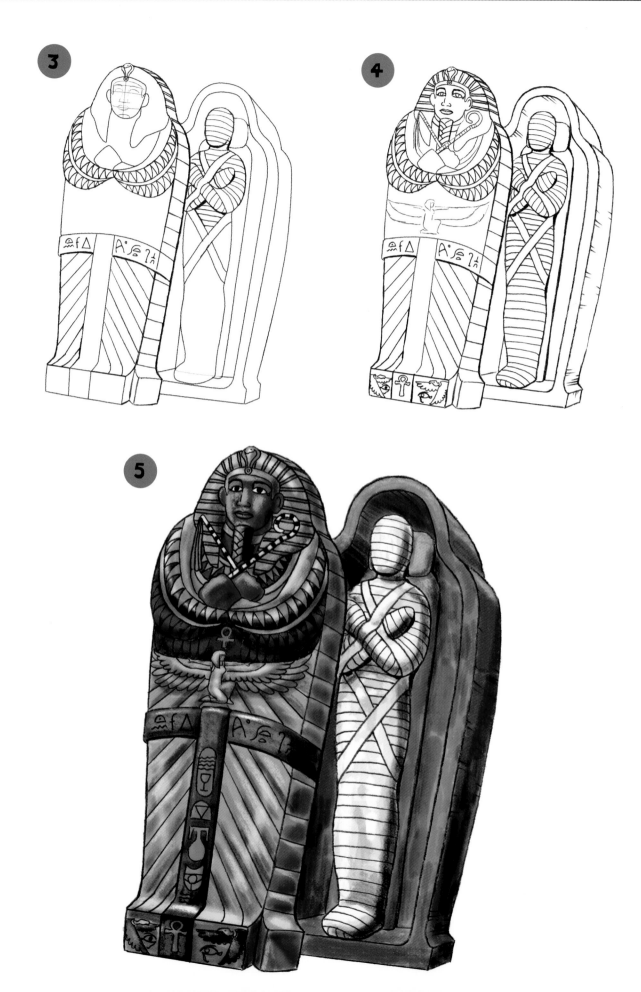

PHARAOH

A pharaoh was a ruler of ancient Egypt. Egyptians believed that pharaohs were half-human and half-god.

FUN FACT

Ancient Egyptians did not call their rulers pharaohs. The word "pharaoh" comes from the Greek language. It means "great house" and was originally used to describe a palace. Some believe the word comes from the Egyptian words *phe*, or "the," and *Ra*, meaning "sun," or "sun god."

4

5

6

DRAWING TIP

You can stylize the Pharaoh's royal clothes using any colors and designs.

LIGHTHOUSE OF ALEXANDRIA

The Lighthouse of Alexandria was the first lighthouse ever built. It stood on the island of Pharos in Egypt and guided sailors with its firelight and smoke.

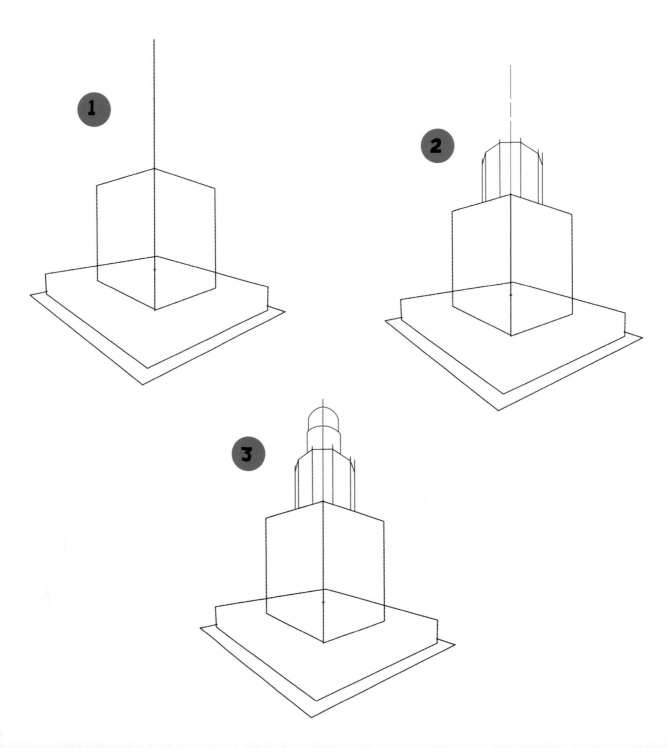

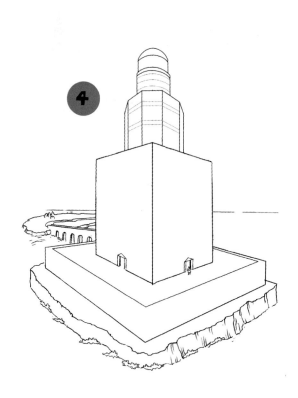

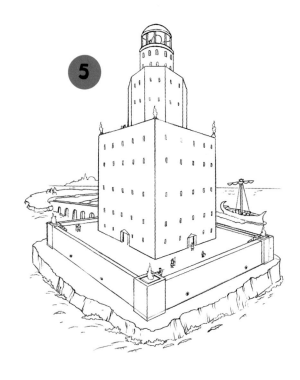

HORUS STATUE

Horus is an ancient Egyptian god. He often appears as a man with the head of a falcon.

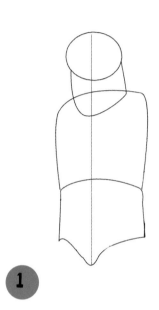

1

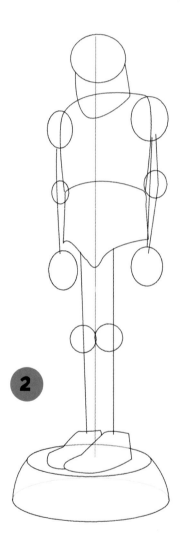

2

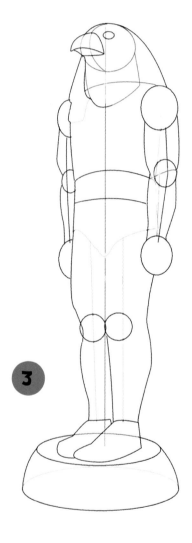

3

FUN FACT

Egyptians believed a king was the living form of Horus. Many statues show pharaohs as either the god Horus or with a falcon above their heads.

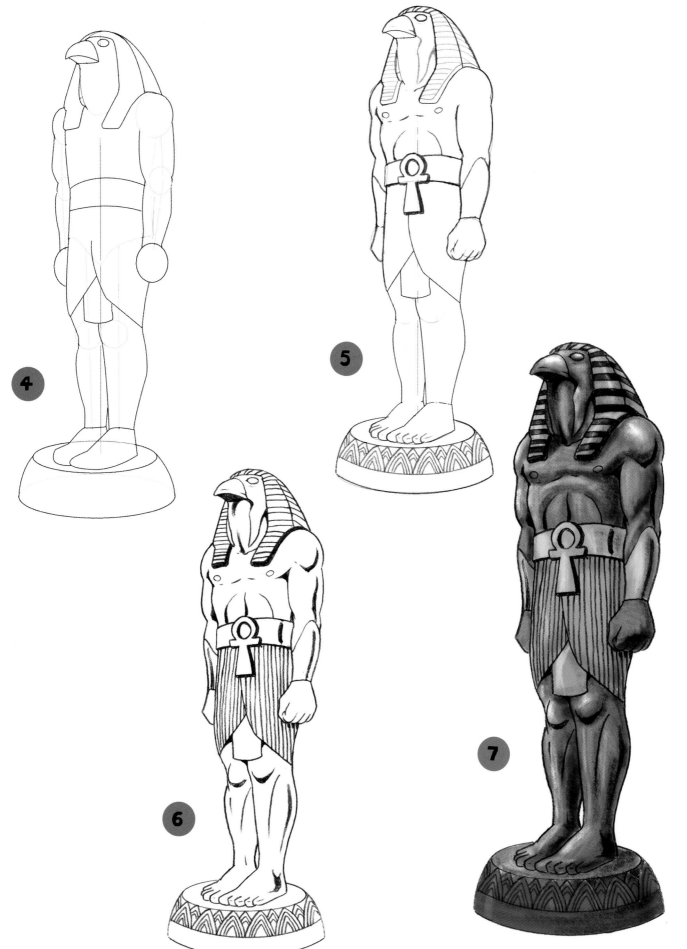

23

CHARIOT

A chariot was a wooden cart with an open back and two wheels. Horses pulled the chariot in battle.

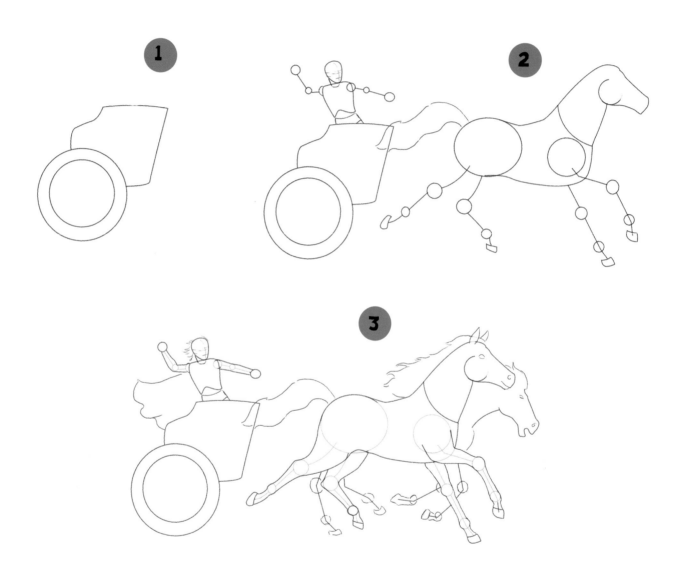

FUN FACT

Chariot racing was a popular Greek and Roman sport. Ancient Olympic games included two- and four-horse chariot races.

HERCULES

Hercules is a mythological, or imaginary, figure who was the son of the Greek god Zeus and a human woman. According to mythological legend, Hercules became a god after he died.

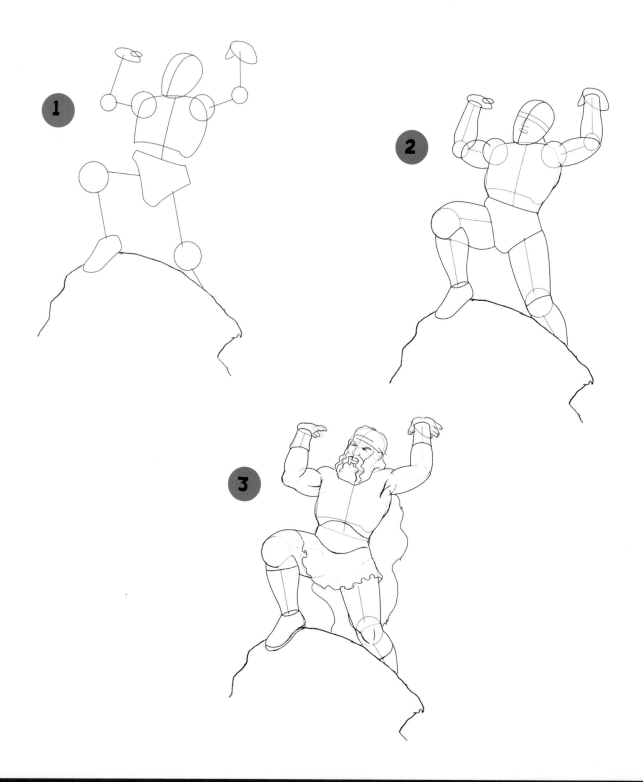

COLOSSUS OF RHODES

The Colossus of Rhodes was a giant statue of the sun god Helios. It stood on the ancient Greek island of Rhodes.

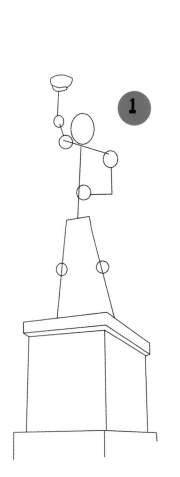

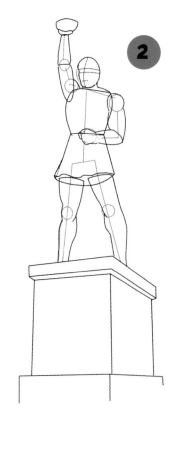

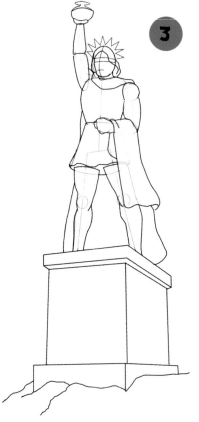

FUN FACT

Many drawings show the Colossus of Rhodes with his legs spanning the harbor entrance. People believed that ships passed beneath his legs; however, engineers say this is impossible. The statue most likely stood to one side of the harbor. It inspired the builders of the Statue of Liberty in New York Harbor.

GLADIATOR

"Gladiator" is the Latin word for "swordsman."
Ancient Romans enjoyed watching gladiators fight—
sometimes to the death!

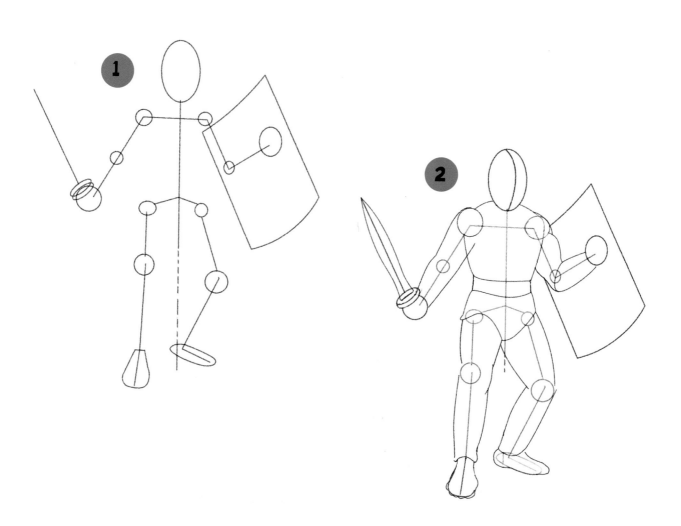

FUN FACT

Most gladiators were slaves who were forced to fight. Spartacus was a famous slave who escaped a gladiatorial training school to return to his homeland, Thrace. Thousands of gladiators and slaves joined him. He led the Gladiatorial War against Rome that lasted for two years. Sadly, Spartacus never made it home.

MAYAN TEMPLE

Mayan temples were built on top of stone pyramids. Steps on the outside of this pyramid led up to the temple.

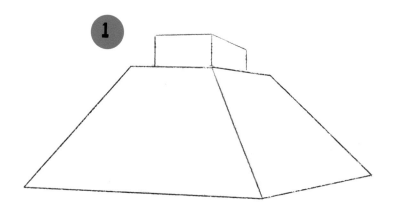

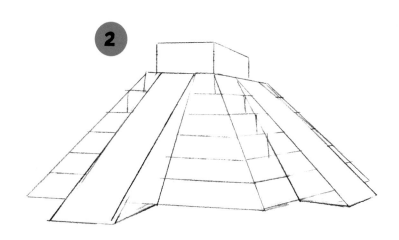

FUN FACT

The Maya built their pyramids and temples based on the movement of the earth, moon, sun, and stars. On the spring and fall equinoxes, when day and night each last 12 hours, you can see an amazing shadow on the temple of Kukulcan in Mexico. It looks like a snake slithering down the staircase.

MAYAN KING

The Maya believed that their kings acted as go-betweens for gods and humans.

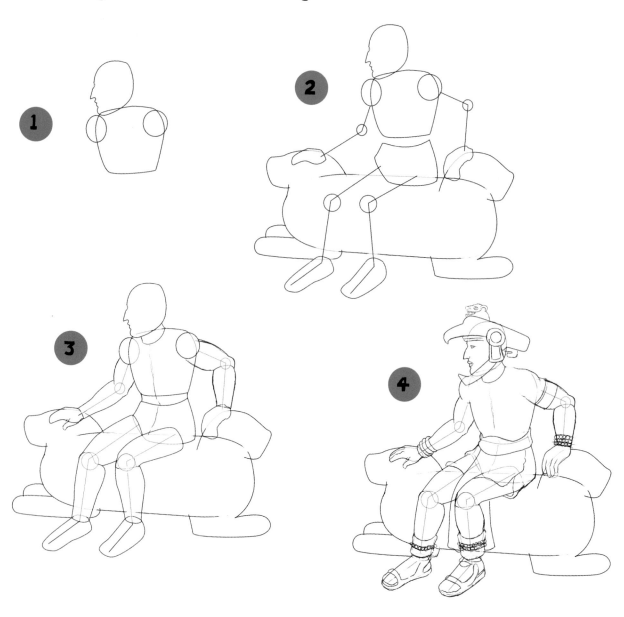

FUN FACT

Math and astronomy were very important to the Maya. These ancient people kept complex calendars and worshipped the sun god and other nature gods.

5

DRAWING TIP

Use stripes, squiggles, polka dots, and other shapes to embellish your Mayan King.

6

CASTLE

Kings and their families lived in medieval castles. These castles were built with thick stone walls to keep enemies out.

FUN FACT

Every part of a castle was designed to protect the people inside. Most castles sat atop a hill, making it easy to see attackers coming. Moats around the castle were filled with water and traps to stop enemies from swimming across. If attackers made it into the castle, spiral staircases with uneven steps tripped them up. The king and his people had plenty of time to hide or escape through secret passages.

KNIGHT

Knights were brave warriors on horseback. They were weapons experts who wore heavy armor in battle.

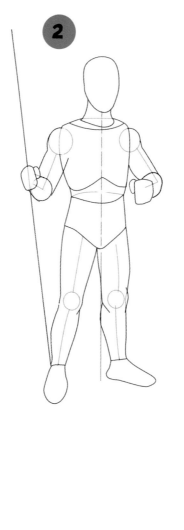

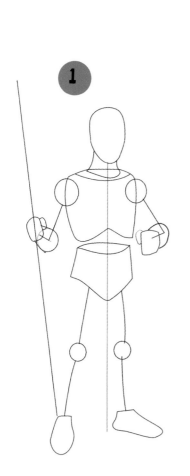

FUN FACT

The path to knighthood was long and hard. Boys, called pages, started training at age seven. They learned how to fight, ride a horse, and practice good manners. At 15, a page became a squire and was assigned to help a knight. A squire who proved himself in battle became a knight.

SWORD IN THE STONE

According to legend, Arthur pulled out a sword that was magically stuck in a stone. This proved he was the rightful king of Britain.

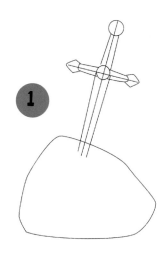

1

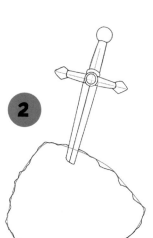

2

3

4

FUN FACT

Many people confuse the sword in the stone with Excalibur, but they were two different weapons. The Lady of the Lake gave King Arthur the magical sword Excalibur, and he used it to win many battles. Before he died, Arthur asked his loyal knight to throw Excalibur back into the lake. A hand rose from the water to catch the sword, and then disappeared.